Riotous Rhymes

Start Students on the Road to Reading
with the Fun of Working with Rhymes

by
Kathryn Wheeler

illustrated by
Janet Armbrust

Little Miss Mungle
Went to the jungle
To find a spider rare.
Along came an ape
And gave her a grape,
While a toucan sat
and stared!

Publisher
Key Education Publishing Company, LLC
Minneapolis, Minnesota

CONGRATULATIONS ON YOUR PURCHASE OF A KEY EDUCATION PRODUCT!

The editors at Key Education are former teachers who bring experience, enthusiasm, and quality to each and every product. Thousands of teachers have looked to the staff at Key Education for new and innovative resources to make their work more enjoyable and rewarding. Key Education is committed to developing and publishing educational materials that will assist teachers in building a strong and developmentally appropriate curriculum for young children.

PLAN FOR GREAT TEACHING EXPERIENCES WHEN YOU USE EDUCATIONAL MATERIALS FROM KEY EDUCATION PUBLISHING COMPANY, LLC

Credits
Author: Kathryn Wheeler
Publisher: Sherrill B. Flora
Cover Art: JJ Rudisill
Illustrations: Janet Armbrust
Editors: Diane Folkerts
　　　　George C. Flora
Cover Design: Annette Hollister-Papp
Production: Key Education

Key Education welcomes manuscripts and product ideas from teachers.
For a copy of our submission guidelines, please send a self-addressed, stamped envelope to:
Key Education Publishing Company, LLC
Acquisitions Department
9601 Newton Avenue South
Minneapolis, Minnesota 55431

About the Author

Kathryn Wheeler has worked as a teacher, an educational consultant, and an editor in educational publishing. She has published workbooks, stories, and magazine articles for children. Kate was awarded a Michigan Council for the Arts grant for fiction. She has a B.A. degree in English from Hope College. Kate lives in Michigan with her husband, Don.

Standard Book Number: 1-933052-28-7
Riotous Rhymes
Copyright © 2006 by Key Education Publishing Company, LLC
Minneapolis, Minnesota 55431

Introduction

One of the most important skills in early reading development is the recognition of patterns. The power of word patterns is clear: when a student recognizes a word pattern, such as a word-family member, it is the key that unlocks sight recognition for an entire group of words. One of the best ways to start students on this road to reading mastery is to work with rhyming words. And the big advantage of rhyming words? They're fun! Attuning students to rhyming sounds prepares them for reading in an enjoyable way.

This book offers groups of fun rhymes that connect with other lessons in the classroom: animals, Mother Goose, weather, colors, and special days rhymes. Different types of activities lend variety to the rhyming fun. Act-it-out poems and play/skits bring action and movement to the rhymes. Flannel-board rhymes and stick-puppet rhymes double as story-time events. Choral chants let students connect rhymes with familiar tunes. Finger plays and minibooks create quieter activity times, while still offering rhyming fun! You will also find follow-up activities that extend word-family learning or connect with other curriculum areas. Use this book to help your students start a lifelong love of words and reading.

⊚ Table of Contents ⊚

WHY I BARK!
(An Act-It-Out Poem)

I want to go in!
Students pretend they are jumping up and down in front of a door.

I want to go out!
Students "paddle" at door with their "paws" to show they want to go out.

I bark, bark, bark,
Students bark loudly. Suggested noises: yip, yap, bow-wow, and arf. Encourage a variety!

Then you shout, shout, shout!
Students cover their ears and hunch down, as if they are being scolded.

I'm only barking
Students should raise their hands up in an "explaining" gesture.

To tell you this:
Students point with finger, as if making a point.

I want a walk.
Students bounce around like they are puppies excited about going on a walk.

I want a kiss.
Students pretend to leap up and give dog kisses to someone.

I want to run.
Students run a few steps or run in place.

I want to play.
Students jump up and down or pretend to chase something.

I want to stay,
Students press hands together and look up pleadingly.

With you all day.
Students point to teacher or reader of poem.

I want to play
Students pretend to chase or do a "play bow," where they bend and stretch out arms.

Until it's dark.
Students point up to the sky.

That's what I mean,
Students hold out hands and arms in a "summing-up" gesture.

When I bark, bark, bark!
Students bark loudly!

Act-it-Out Poem Directions: Read the poem aloud while students perform the suggested actions.

WHY I BARK! Puppy Mask

Directions: Students can wear this mask for the Act-it-Out poem, "Why I Bark!" Reproduce the mask on card stock for each student. Have the students cut out and color their masks however they wish.

Then carefully cut out the eyeholes and the holes on each edge of the mask. Thread yarn or shoelaces through the holes so that the mask can be gently tied around the back of the head.

Follow-up Activity

Ask the students to draw a picture of a dog that they have always wanted. Put the drawings in a classroom book called *Dog Dreams*.

TWINKLE, TWINKLE LITTLE PIG

(A Choral Chant)

Twinkle, twinkle, little pig!

You are pink and you are big.

How I wonder what you eat,

Corn and clover, plums and beets!

Twinkle, twinkle, little pig!

You are pink and you are big.

Choral Chant Directions

First teach the words of "Twinkle, Twinkle Little Pig" to the students. Then have everyone sing the song to the tune of "Twinkle, Twinkle Little Star."

Follow-up Activity

Have a pet pig-naming contest! Encourage the students to think up funny names for their pigs. Help them write the selected choices on name tags for their pets.

TWINKLE, TWINKLE: Pet Pigs for Everybody!

You will need: Sheets of cardboard; two spring-action clothespins per student; one pipe cleaner per student (optional); pink crayons or paint.

Directions: Use the pattern below to cut out a cardboard pig shape for each student. Have the students color and draw faces on their pigs. Punch a hole for each pig's pipe cleaner tail. Have students thread the tail through the hole and wind it around a pencil to get a curly tail. *(Alternative: draw a tail in black crayon or marker.)* Attach one clothespin for the front legs and one for the back legs.

LITTLE BEAR
(A Play/Skit)

First person: Little bear, little bear, where are you going?

Little Bear: I'm going outside where it is snowing!

Second person: Little bear, little bear, you should be asleep!

Little Bear: But my alarm just went, "Beep, beep, beep."

Third person: Little bear, little bear, your bed is soft and nice.

Little Bear: But I want to play in the snow and the ice!

Fourth person: Little bear, little bear, close your eyes again.

Little Bear: I'll go back to sleep now in my nice, warm den.

Play/Skit Directions
This can be acted out as a play or read as a "readers' theater" poem. The teacher can take the part of Little Bear, or assign the part to a student with a good memory. Student actors may alternate reading the remaining lines. For nonreaders, a visual script has been included on page 8.

Follow-up Activity
Share a bedtime snack to help Little Bear get back to sleep. How about instant hot cocoa and honey graham crackers? While the students enjoy the snack, talk about hibernation.

LITTLE BEAR: Script for Nonreaders

Directions: This picture-based script will help nonreaders remember their lines.

First Person: Little bear, little bear, where are you going?

Little Bear: I'm going outside where it is snowing!

Second Person: Little bear, little bear, you should be asleep!

 Beep! Beep! Beep!

Little Bear: But my alarm just went, "Beep, beep, beep."

Third Person: Little bear, little bear, your bed is soft and nice.

Little Bear: But I want to play in the snow and the ice!

Fourth Person: Little bear, little bear, close your eyes again.

Little Bear: I'll go back to sleep now in my nice, warm den.

ROCK-A-BYE, LITTLE SQUIRREL
(A Flannel-Board Rhyme)

Rock-a-bye, little squirrel, in the tree top.

When the wind blows, your nest, it will rock.

When the bough shakes, the acorns will drop,

After you eat them, off you will hop!

Rock-a-bye, little squirrel, looking for treats.

Acorns and walnuts, seeds you can eat.

When it gets dark, climb back to your nest,

And sleep until morning, the time you love best!

Flannel-Board Rhyme Directions

Read this rhyme aloud or sing the words to the tune of "Rock-a-Bye Baby," as you use pieces on the flannel board to reinforce different vocabulary words. Flannel-board patterns and complete directions can be found on page 10.

Follow-up Activity

Play some acorn games! Acorns are great objects to use for counting games. You can paint tiny squirrel faces on acorns for a craft idea. You can also use a hot-glue gun to help students create patterns with acorn caps on fiberboard or cardboard. Another idea is to use the acorn caps and acorns as Xs and Os for tic-tac-toe.

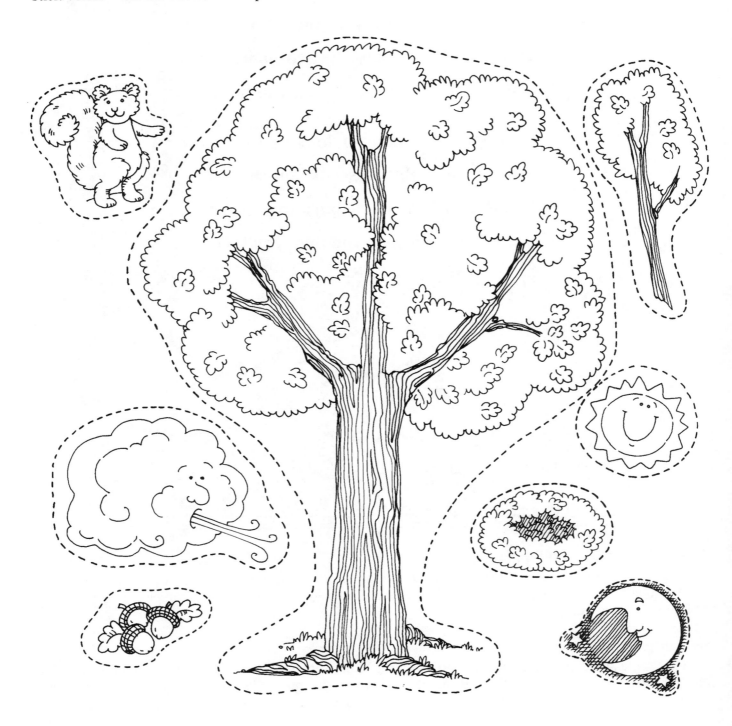

ROCK-A-BYE, LITTLE SQUIRREL:
Flannel-Board Patterns

Directions: Use these patterns to make flannel-board storytelling pieces for the rhyme. Copy the patterns onto card stock, color, cut-out, and laminate for durability. Then glue sandpaper or place self-stick Velcro™ on the back of each pattern.

THE GIRAFFE'S DINNER

(A Choral Chant)

**Does the giraffe
Make you laugh?
Her neck is long and hollow.
While she eats,
Please take your seats—
It takes two days to swallow!**

Choral Chant Directions

First teach the words of the song to the students and then have everyone sing the song to the tune of "Jack and Jill Went Up the Hill."

Follow-up Activity

Make a giraffe puppet. Paint a paper-towel tube yellow with brown spots. Draw a giraffe face by using the pictures below as a guide. Color and cut out the face. Glue the face to the top of the tube.

Learn About Giraffes

Copy this sheet for each student. Use the facts listed below as discussion starters about real-life giraffes. Invite the students to color the pictures.

Giraffes have long necks!
This helps them eat leaves from
the tops of trees.

Giraffes make sounds.
They whistle, hiss, and moo
like cows!

Giraffes have big eyes.
They have long eyelashes!

Giraffes use baby-sitters!
One giraffe watches all
the babies.

Giraffe fur comes
in many different patterns.

Giraffes help each other.
One giraffe watches out while
the others drink.

LION AND MOUSE

(A Stick-Puppet Rhyme)

Why would the lion
Be sitting and crying?
He wishes he was a mouse!
"If I was small,
I could run down a hall,
And live in the floor of a house!"

Why would the mouse
Sit and grouse?
He wishes he was a lion!
"If I were brave,
I could live in a cave,
And roar instead of sighing!"

Stick-Puppet Rhyme Directions

Stick-puppet patterns can be found on pages 12 and 13. Copy, color, and cut out the patterns. Attach each figure to a craft stick using glue or double-sided tape. Use the puppets to act out the poem.

Follow-up Activity

Talk about how people sometimes wish they were different. What do the students like about themselves? What would they like to do differently or what skills would they like to learn?

Stick-Puppet Patterns

LION AND MOUSE: Stick-Puppet Patterns

BUILDING A WEB (A Finger Play)

One little spider said, "Let's build a home!"

Two little spiders said, "How about a dome?"

Three little spiders said, "Silly! That's for bees!"

Four little spiders said, "A web will be a breeze."

Five little spiders came to help the others spin.

They spun a great big web and then they all moved in!

Finger Play Directions

Read the poem aloud while the students hold up the correct number of fingers for each line.

Follow-up Activity

Make spider mobiles. Paint paper plates black and then add red construction-paper eyes. Staple eight black crepe-paper streamers to each plate for legs. Hang the completed spiders in a window.

BUILDING A WEB: Spider Sorting Activity

Directions: Here are the little spiders from the poem! See how many different ways students can sort the spiders. Copy and cut them out. Make two sorting circles with long pieces of yarn. Have students talk about the spider pictures and sort and re-sort according to attributes (smiling or not smiling; wearing a hat or not; wearing shoes or not.) If you want to add another attribute to the sorting, add spot color to each picture, using two different colors. After the students sort for each attribute, ask them to count the number of spiders in each set.

TWO LITTLE BIRDS
(An Act-It-Out/Puppet Poem)

Two little birds came and sat on my head.
Students "fly" their fingers toward their hair.

I said, "Please, little birds, find a tree instead!"
Students shake their fingers as if lecturing.

The two little birds said, "You have such curly hair."
Students "fluff out" hair with fingers.

We saw it and we said, "Let's build a nest in there."
Students hold hands in a circle to indicate a nest.

I said, "I'd love to watch you build a little nest,
Students put hands over hearts.

But please, please, little birds! A tree would be best!"
Students clasp hands in appeal.

Act-it-Out Poem Directions
Read the poem aloud while the students perform the suggested actions. Copy, color, and cut out each pattern below. Attach each figure to a craft stick using glue or double-sided tape. Use the puppets to act out the poem.

Follow-up Activity
Bring in a book about birds that shows different kinds of nests. Talk about how birds build their nests.

Stick-Puppet Patterns

RABBIT HOLIDAY
(A Stick-Puppet Rhyme)

I asked Dad, "What's for lunch?"

He said, "Carrots, by the bunch!

Here's a big, red, juicy beet,

And some lettuce for a treat.

Now we have all that we need."

We all yelled, "Hop, hop hooray!

It's time for Rabbit Picnic Day!"

Stick-Puppet Rhyme Directions

Use the stick puppets to help tell the story of this poem. Patterns can be found on pages 16 and 17. Copy, color, and cut out each pattern. (Reproduce as many "child" rabbits as you like.) Attach each figure to a craft stick by using glue or double-sided tape.

Follow-up Activity

Talk about holidays. What holidays do the students like best? Why?

Stick Puppet Patterns

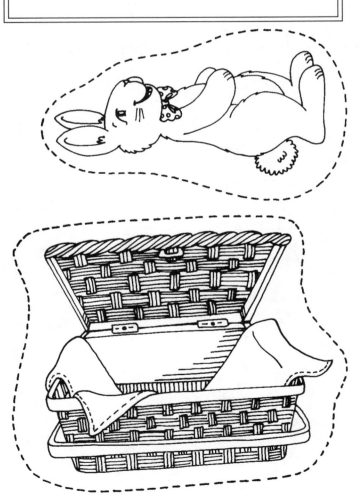

RABBIT HOLIDAY: Stick-Puppet Patterns

RABBIT PICNIC

THE TEENY TINY ANT
(A Minibook Poem)

The teeny tiny, itty bitty, eensy weensy ant
Went for a picnic on the GREAT BIG plant.

There he met a spider with GREAT BIG eyes
Who said, "Little ant! You look as tasty as a pie!"

The teeny tiny, itty bitty, eensy weensy ant
Said, "I'll just hop along now to a brand-new plant!"

There he had his eensy weensy, teeny tiny lunch
Of itty bitty bread crumbs that he munched and munched!

Directions: Read this poem to the students before they begin work on their minibooks. Copy pages 18, 19, and 20 for each student. Have the students color, cut out, and staple the pages together in numerical order.

THE TEENY TINY ANT

This minibook
belongs to:

_____

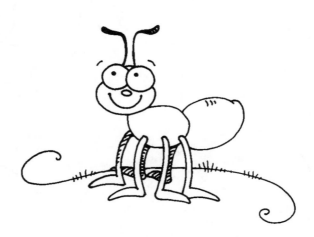

The teeny tiny, itty bitty,
eensy weensy ant

-1-

Went for a picnic on a
GREAT BIG plant.

-2-

There he met a spider with
GREAT BIG eyes.

-3-

Who said, "Little ant!
You look as tasty as a pie!"

-4-

The teeny tiny, itty bitty,
eensy weensy ant

-5-

Said, "I'll just hop along now
to a brand-new plant!"
-6-

There he had his eensy weensy,
teeny tiny lunch.
-7-

Of itty bitty bread crumbs that he
munched and munched!
-8-

Follow-up Activities

1. Invite ants to a picnic! Give each student a paper placemat or a piece of construction paper. Have the students find pictures of their favorite foods to cut out and glue onto their placemats. Then ask them to draw their ant guests on the placemat, marching toward a big picnic meal!

2. Eat "ants on plants" snacks! Make celery stick snacks with peanut butter filling. Add raisin "ants" to the peanut butter and enjoy.

3. Purchase or borrow an ant farm and have the students observe real ants in action.

4. Feed some neighborhood ants. Put together a plate with various ant "treats." You can try graham cracker crumbs, small pieces of lettuce, and a few ground-up peanuts. Place the plate outside in an area on your playground, or near your classroom, where you've seen ant activity. Allow the students to check the plate after a few hours. Have the ants found their treats? What do they seem to like the best?

(**Note of Caution:** Always be aware of students who have peanut allergies.)

FIVE HEALTHY PIGS
(An Act-It-Out Poem)

This little piggy had a salad,
Students pretend to eat something with a fork.

This little piggy lifted weights,
Students bend down, pretend to pick up weights, and lift them.

This little piggy drank some water,
Students lean heads back and pretend to drink from a glass.

This little piggy ate some dates,
Students pretend to toss dates in the air and catch them in their mouths.

And this little piggy went jog, jog, jog,
Students jog in place.

All the way home!

Act-It-Out Poem Directions: Read the poem aloud while the students perform the suggested actions.

Follow-up Activity

Reproduce the Healthy Habits Chart found on page 22 for each student. Record the students progress as they keep track of their healthy habits.

FIVE HEALTHY PIGS: Healthy Habits Chart

Directions: Reproduce and hand out to the students for coloring and discussion.

Drink lots of water every day.

Walk to the store.

Eat fruits and vegetables.

Play outside!

Wash your hands before meals.

Get lots of rest.

A TRIP TO THE MALL
(A Choral Chant)

Jill and Paul

Went to the mall

To buy a new computer.

Jill took it home,

Packed up in foam.

Paul followed on his scooter!

Choral Chant Directions
First teach the words of the rhyme to the students and then have everyone sing, "A Trip to the Mall," to the tune of "Jack and Jill Went Up the Hill."

Stick-Puppet Patterns
Copy, color, and cut out each pattern below. Attach each figure to a craft stick using glue or double-sided tape. Use the puppets to act out the poem.

Follow-up Activity
What are your students' favorite computer games or activities? If you have a computer in your classroom, see if you can find a site with an interactive version of "Jack and Jill" or one that plays the nursery rhyme music.

A TRIP TO THE MALL: Stick-Puppet Patterns

RUB-A-DUB CLUCK!
(A Flannel-Board Poem)

Rub-a-dub cluck,

Three hens and a duck,

Where do you think they might be?

In a tub with a sail—

They will have quite a tale

When they cluck and quack over the sea!

Flannel-Board Poem Directions

Read this poem aloud as you use the pieces on the flannel board to reinforce different vocabulary words. The flannel-board patterns can be found on pages 24 and 25. Use a marker to write "Quack!" and "Cluck!" in the two cartoon balloons. Copy the patterns onto card stock, color, cut out, and laminate for durability. Then glue sandpaper or place self-stick Velcro™ on the back of each pattern.

Follow-up Activity

You can make your own sailing "tubs" with small paper cups and construction-paper sails. Use small, colored pom-poms to make hens and ducks to go in the tubs! Or fill the boats with candy chicks and ducks.

Flannel-Board Patterns

RUB-A-DUB CLUCK: Flannel-Board Patterns

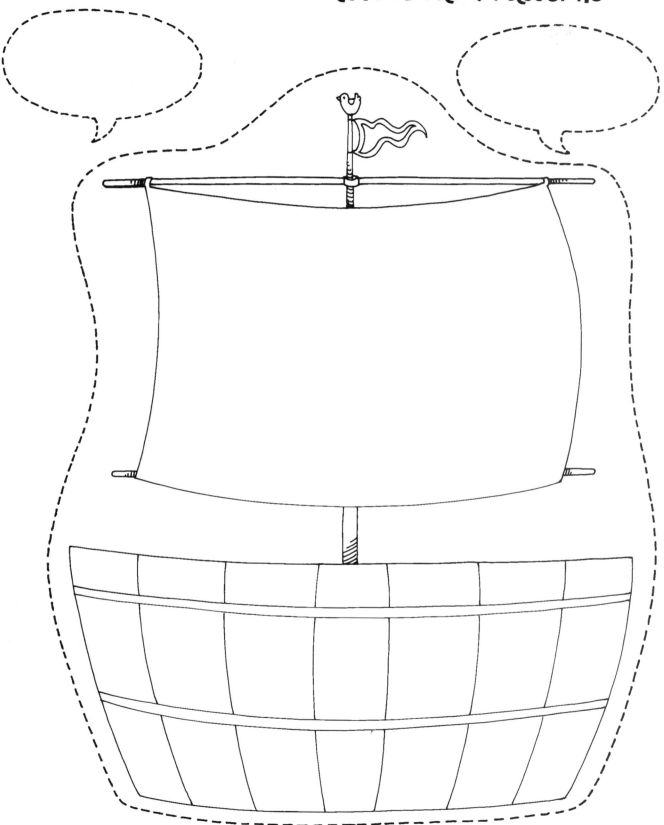

HICKORY, DICKORY, DOCK

(An Act-It-Out Poem)

Hickory, Dickory, Dock
Students pretend to be clocks, with moving clock hands.

The mouse found his lost sock.
Students point to one of their socks.

The clock struck one,
Students hold up one finger.

It's time to run!
Students run in place.

Hickory, Dickory, Dock.
Students pretend to be clocks, with moving clock hands.

Hickory, Dickory, Dace,
Students pretend to be clocks, with moving clock hands.

The mouse is in a race.
Students bend over into a starting position, then run in place.

The clock struck two;
Students hold up two fingers.

He won! Yahoo!
Students jump up and down and cheer.

Hickory, Dickory, Dace.
Students pretend to be clocks, with moving clock hands.

Act-It-Out Directions

Teach the students the words to the rhyme and the suggested actions.

Follow-Up Activity

Use the "Time and Rhyme" reproducible activity on page 27 to help reinforce the concepts of "rhyming" and "time."

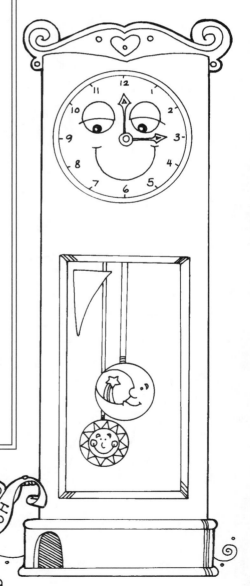

Theme: Madcap Mother Goose

HICKORY, DICKORY, DOCK: Time and Rhyme Activity

Directions: Use the rhyme as a springboard to talk about time. What time of the day do the students do specific things? Use the mouse cards below to start a discussion about each type of activity and what time it occurs. Use the two blank cards to make up your own rhymes with your class.

Hickory, Dickory, Deal.
It's time for the mouse's meal.

Hickory, Dickory, Deed.
It's time for the mouse to read.

Hickory, Dickory, Day.
It's time for the mouse to play.

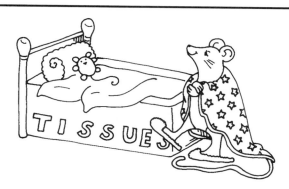

Hickory, Dickory, Deep.
It's time for the mouse to sleep.

Hickory, Dickory, _____.
It's time for the mouse to _____.

Hickory, Dickory, _____.
It's time for the mouse to _____.

JACK BE SPEEDY

(A Stick-Puppet Rhyme)

Jack be speedy,

Jack be fast.

Jack in his race car,

Roaring past!

Stick-Puppet Rhyme Directions

Use the stick-puppet patterns below to help tell the story of this poem. Copy, color, and cut out each pattern. Attach each figure to a craft stick using glue or double-sided tape. Use the puppets to act out the poem. Ask students questions: "Is Jack in a race? Is he winning? Who sees Jack roaring past? What might happen next?"

Follow-up Activity

Have students draw pictures of race cars. Invite them to decorate their cars however they like, using their favorite colors and writing their names on the side of the cars.

JACK BE SPEEDY: Stick-Puppet Patterns

LITTLE MISS MUNGLE
(Choral Chant)

Little Miss Mungle

Went to the jungle

To find a spider rare.

Along came an ape

And gave her a grape,

While a toucan sat and stared!

Choral Chant Directions

Read this poem aloud, emphasizing the rhythm. Teach the words to the students. Students can clap their hands or stamp their feet to the rhythm of the poem as they chant the words together.

Follow-up Activity

Make a rain forest snack for Little Miss Mungle: curds and whey (cottage cheese) with cashews, chocolate chips, bananas or banana chips, or other fruit stirred in.

Learn More about Spiders

Copy page 30 for each student. Follow the directions on the page.

LITTLE MISS MUNGLE: Stick-Puppet Patterns

LITTLE MISS MUNGLE: Learn about Spiders!

Directions: What kind of rare spider was Miss Mungle looking for? Copy this page for each student and talk about these fun spider facts.

Spiders have eight legs.

Spiders have eight eyes, too.

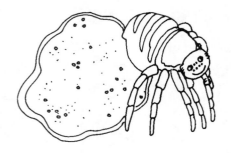

Big spiders can lay
8,000 eggs at one time.

Wolf spiders are very strong.

Crab spiders walk sideways.

Fishing spiders can run
on the top of the water.

PUSSYCAT, PUSSYCAT
(A Play/Skit)

First person:	Pussycat, pussycat!
Second person:	Where have you been?
Pussycat:	I've been to Saturn and came back again.
Third person:	Pussycat, pussycat!
Fourth person:	What did you do?
Pussycat:	I built a space station for cats—and mice, too!

Play/Skit Directions

This can be acted out as a play or read as a "readers' theater" poem. The teacher can take the part of the Pussycat, or a student with a good memory can be assigned that part. Student actors may alternate reading the remaining lines. For nonreaders, a visual script has been included on page 32.

Follow-up Activity

Play "cat and mice"! Organize a game of hide-and-seek. The person who is "it" is the cat. The other students are the mice and they all go and hide. The last mouse caught becomes the cat for the next round.

Pussycat, Pussycat: Script for Nonreaders

Directions: This picture-based script will help nonreaders remember their lines.

First Person: Pussycat, Pussycat!

Second Person: Where have you been?

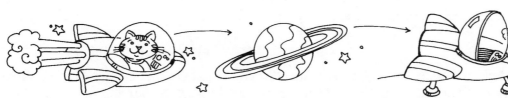

Pussycat: I've been to Saturn and came back again.

Third Person: Pussycat, Pussycat!

Fourth Person: What did you do?

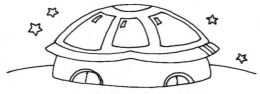 

Pussycat: I built a space station for cats—and mice, too!

A DILLAR, A DOLLAR

(A Choral Chant)

Medium voices: **A dillar, a dollar,**

Low voices: **A space rocket scholar,**

High voices: **She's flying to the stars!**

Low voices: **She used to just go to the moon,**

All voices: **But now she goes to Mars!**

Choral Chant Directions

This choral chant uses different types of voices to make "music." Sort your students by the range of their voices. Then perform the poem for a choral reading experience. Assign the appropriate lines for each group to memorize.

A DILLAR, A DOLLAR: Rhyming Riddles

Directions: To reinforce the learning of rhyming words, tell these fun "outer space" riddles and explain to your students that the answers have to rhyme. Use the word cards found on page 34 to reinforce the visual learning of the words.

1. What can you drive on Mars?

   Mars _____

2. What do you use to hold your star collection?

   A star _____

3. What do you call a race from one planet to another?

   A _____ race

4. What do you use to eat your soup on the moon?

   A moon _____

5. What piece of jewelry can you wear on a space trip?

   A rocket _____

cars

jar

space

spoon

locket

OLD MOTHER MYRTLE

(A Stick-Puppet Rhyme)

Old Mother Myrtle
Rode off on her turtle,
To buy her poor dog a bone.
Her trip was so slow,
Her dog baked bread dough
From wheat that he'd planted and grown!

Stick-Puppet Directions

Use the stick-puppet patterns below to help tell the story of this poem. Copy, color, and cut out each pattern. Attach each figure to a craft stick using glue or double-sided tape. Ask the students questions: "How slow is a turtle? How long does it take to grow wheat? How long has Old Mother Myrtle been gone? What might happen next?"

Follow-up Activity

Make Mother Myrtle's turtle! Find round, flat pebbles and paint them green. Glue on green construction paper heads and legs.

Stick-Puppet Patterns

ONE, TWO, BOO!
(A Minibook Poem)

One, two,
Tom said, "Boo!"

Three, four,
He scared Flor.

Five, six,
She spilled cake mix!

Seven, eight,
Which slipped up Kate.

Nine, ten,
She slid into Ben!

What a mess!
Look at Flor's dress!

Help Kate get up.
Pick up that cup!

Let's scrub the floor,
And clean up you four,

Before we bake
Another cake!

Minibook Directions: Read this poem to the students before they begin work on their minibooks. Copy pages 36, 37, and 38 for each student. Have the students color, cut out, and staple the pages together in numerical order.

ONE, TWO, BOO!

This minibook belongs

to: _____

One, two,
Tom said, "Boo!"

-1-

Three, four,
He scared Flor.

-2-

Five, six,
She spilled cake mix!

-3-

Seven, eight,
Which slipped up Kate.

-4-

Nine, ten,
She slid into Ben!

-5-

**What a mess!
Look at Flor's dress!**

-6-

**Help Kate get up.
Pick up that cup!**

-7-

**Let's scrub the floor,
And clean up you four,
Before we bake another cake.**

-8-

Follow-up Activities

1. Have the students draw pictures of cakes they would like to make. Ask each student what would be needed to make the cake in their drawing.

2. Provide or ask the students to bring in cupcakes and decorations—sprinkles, colored sugar, etc. Decorate your "minicakes" and enjoy!

3. Take a vote on everybody's favorite kind of cake. Be sure to vote on both cake and frosting flavors. Create a bar chart that shows the results of your vote.

4. Make a "cake" for the birds in your schoolyard! You can use pinecones rolled in peanut butter and sunflower seeds. Or you can buy a commercially made suet cake and "decorate" it with seeds and peanut butter. Make time to watch and see if your cake gets eaten!

(**Note of Caution:** Always be aware of students who have peanut allergies.)

SNOW THOUGHTS
(An Act-It-Out Poem)

When you jump in the snow,
Students jump
Where do you go?
Hold up their hands looking puzzled.
You might end up
In Mexico—

In Mexico
Where, you know,
There's hardly ever
Any snow!
Students shake their heads for "no."

You might end up
In bright Niger,
Students shade their eyes as if it is sunny.
Too hot in all
Your winter gear.
Students fan themselves with their hands.

You could end up
In cold Norway,
Students hug themselves and shiver.
Where you are dressed
Just right for play!
Students jump up and down in the snow.

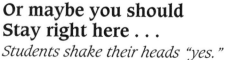

Or maybe you should
Stay right here . . .
Students shake their heads "yes."
Let's play in the snow, my dear, my dear.
Students pretend to play in the snow
—throwing snowballs, making snowmen.

Act-It-Out Poem Directions
Read aloud the poem while the students perform the suggested actions.

Follow-up Activities
Find these countries on a map. Talk about how weather varies in different parts of the world. Complete the reproducible activity, "Snow Thoughts: Learn about Other Countries," found on page 40.

SNOW THOUGHTS: Learn about Other Countries

Directions: Where can you "jump in the snow" and go? Learn about three countries and then add information about your own country!

Mexico is bright and sunny.
It has spicy foods
and beautiful beaches.

Niger is a desert country.
It has a big wildlife park
in the south.

Norway is in the far north.
It has mountains and forests
and lots of snow!

My country is

_____.
Here is my house.

THE BIG STORM
(A Choral Chant)

High voices:	The wind talked to me all night long.
Low voices:	It said, "You are small and I am strong."
Medium voices:	It rattled my window. It pushed at the door.
Low voices:	Then I fell asleep and heard no more.
High voices:	This morning, the sky is bright and clear.
All voices (shouting quote):	I shout, "You are gone and I'M STILL HERE!"

Choral Chant Directions

This choral chant uses different types of voices to make "music." Sort your students by the range of their voices. Then assign the appropriate lines for each group to memorize. You can direct the poem like a piece of music.

Follow-up Activities

Make up conversations with other kinds of weather. What does the weather say to the students and what do they want to say back to the weather? On page 42 you will find the reproducible activity, "The Big Storm: Weather Talk." Complete the activity to encourage oral language usage and help the students learn more about the weather.

THE BIG STORM: Weather Talk

Theme: Wacky Weather

Directions: Does the weather have something to say to us? Enlarge and reproduce the cards below. Ask the students: What would each kind of weather say if it could talk? Read each set of dialogue lines out loud. You can play a matching/guessing game or have students make up their own lines for each type of weather. Challenge them to make up rhyming lines.

sunny day

clear night

rain

snow

"Is my <u>light</u> too <u>bright</u>?"

"I'll <u>warm</u> you <u>up</u>!"

"I'm a <u>sign</u> to <u>shine</u>!"

"I'll <u>light</u> your <u>night</u>."

"Do you like the stars around me?"

"I'm a <u>white</u> <u>light</u>."

"Just <u>try</u> to stay <u>dry</u>!"

"<u>I</u> flow and help things <u>grow</u>."

"Splash!"

"Brrrr!"

"Want to <u>play</u> <u>today</u>?"

"Stay <u>warm</u> in this <u>storm</u>!"

HOT, HOT, HOT!
(A Flannel-Board Rhyme)

What can you do
When it's hot, hot, hot?
Watch your dog pant a lot,
Lie in the shade,
Drink lemonade,
Eat a peach,
Go to the beach,
And dig in the wet, cool sand a lot!

Flannel-Board Rhyme Directions

Read this poem aloud as you use the pieces on the flannel board to reinforce different vocabulary words. Copy the patterns found on pages 43 and 44 onto card stock, color, cut out, and laminate for durability. Then glue sandpaper or place self-stick Velcro™ on the back of each pattern.

Follow-up Activity

Make frozen treats for a sweet reminder of summertime! Pour juice into small paper cups. Wait until the juice is soft and slushy (about two hours), then add sticks or plastic spoons into the cups. Return them to the freezer overnight. Once frozen, tear off the paper cups and enjoy!

Flannel-Board Patterns

HOT, HOT, HOT! Flannel-Board Patterns

WHAT'S THE WEATHER IN OUTER SPACE?
(A Finger Play)

On other planets, is there snow?
Students wiggle fingers to indicate "snow."

Do they have rain? I just don't know!
Students hold up their hands in puzzlement.

Maybe their snow is pink and gold;
Students put fingers on chins to show they are thinking.

Maybe it isn't even cold.
Students fan themselves with their hands.

Maybe their rain falls up, not down.
Students point up in the air.

Maybe it only falls in town.
Students point away from themselves, to "town."

Maybe there is no rain or snow,
Students shake heads.

I wonder, but I just don't know!

Finger Play Directions
Read the rhyme aloud while the students pantomime the actions.

Follow-up Activity
Do you have special weather in your part of the world that other people might not have? What are the strangest kinds of weather that you've heard about? Draw pictures!

Art Activity
Let each of the students draw a picture of a rainy day on some other planet. Encourage creative thinking. When the drawings are finished, dot the picture with drops of white glue. Then sprinkle multicolored glitter on the glue to create colorful rain on the students' imaginary planets!

Alternative idea with less mess: Create the raindrops with a glitter glue pen.

STRANGE RAIN
(An Act-It-Out Poem)

If it rained frogs,
Raindrops would hop!
Students hop around.

If it rained birds,
There'd be wings in each drop.
Students flap their arms like wings.

If it rained lions,
Our raindrops would roar.
Students throw back their heads and roar!

If it rained candy,
We'd wish it rained more!
Students rub their stomachs and smile.

Act-It-Out Poem Directions: Read the poem aloud while the students pantomime the actions.

STRANGE RAIN: Rhyming Riddles

Directions: To reinforce the learning of rhyming words, tell these fun "wacky weather" riddles and explain to your students that the answers have to rhyme. Print the following words on index cards to reinforce visual learning of the words: *snake, flake, worm, squirm, cat, hat, paw, thaw, hop, and drop.*

1. If it snowed snakes, what would each tiny piece of snow be called?

      A snake _____

2. If it rained worms, what could you call a storm?

      A worm _____

3. If it rained kittens, what would you wear outside in the rain?

      A _____ hat

4. If it snowed dogs, what would you call it when it thawed?

      A _____ thaw

5. If it rained rabbits, what would you call the raindrops?

      A _____ drop

FOGGY MORNING ON THE FARM
(A Stick-Puppet or Flannel-Board Rhyme)

In the fog, no one could see.
When the fog cleared—oh my! Oh me!
The little pink hog
Was stuck in a log.
Six little chicks
Had tripped over sticks.
The great big black horse

Had run off his course.
The quack-quacking duck
Was stuck in the muck!
The farmer ran there,
The farmer ran here,
Fixing the mess
On the farm—oh, dear!

Stick-Puppet or Flannel-Board Rhyme Directions

Use the stick-puppet patterns on pages 47, 48, and 49 to help tell the story of this rhyme. To make stick puppets, copy, color, and cut out each pattern. Attach each figure to a craft stick using glue or double-sided tape. To make the flannel-board pieces, copy the patterns onto card stock, color, cut out, and laminate for durability, Then glue sandpaper or place self-stick Velcro™ on the back of each pattern.

Follow-up Activity

Brainstorm lists of word families from the rimes in the poem: -ee, -og, -icks (or –ix), -orse, -uck, and –ear.

Stick-Puppet or Flannel-Board Patterns

FOGGY MORNING ON THE FARM:
Stick-Puppet or
Flannel-Board Patterns

FOGGY MORNING ON THE FARM:
Stick-Puppet or Flannel-Board Patterns

THE FIRST FROST

(A Finger Play)

"Brrr!" said Skip Chipmunk.
"The first frost has come.
Students hug themselves as if they are cold.

It's a red flag to me:
the summer is done!
Students "flick" summer away with one hand.

The frost has left everything
cake-icing white.
Students point around at "everything."

All the leaves sparkle; a shivery sight!
Students make a "sparkly" motion with fingers.

Ouch! The grass crunches under my feet.
*Students "walk" their fingers to show
the chipmunk's feet.*

It's time for me now to find lots to eat!
Students pretend to eat a nut or a piece of fruit.

I'll zip back and forth, I'll be very busy.
Students move fingers back and forth very quickly.

I'll look for more food until I get dizzy.
Students move a finger around in a circle.

I'll stow treats away
in my nest down below,
Students pretend to put something away.

And be fast asleep
when it starts to snow!"
Students put hands under cheek in a sleep gesture.

Finger Play Directions

Read the poem aloud as the students do the finger play.

Follow-up Activities

Talk about hibernation. What would it be like to sleep all winter? What other animals, besides chipmunks, hibernate? Use the reproducible activity found on page 51 to learn more about chipmunks.

THE FIRST FROST: Chipmunks and Weather

Directions: What's the connection between the weather and the life of the chipmunk? Learn these fun chipmunk facts. Have the students color the page.

Warm spring weather wakes up the chipmunks.

In the summer, chipmunks have babies.

Chipmunks carry food in their cheeks.

Chipmunks build homes underground.

Chipmunks begin to store food before it gets too cold.

Chipmunks sleep all winter.

RAIN ON MARS
(A Flannel-Board Rhyme)

When it rains on Mars,
It stops all of the cars,
Because the rain is blue,
And gooey, just like glue!
So if you walk or race,
You get stuck in one place.
When the sun comes out,
Then folks can move about.
That's when they shout, "Hooray!
It's a rain-is-over day!"

Flannel-Board Rhyme Directions

Read this poem aloud as you place pieces on the flannel board to reinforce different vocabulary words. The flannel-board patterns can be found on pages 52 and 53.

Follow-up Activity

Use the flannel-board Martians as counters in a sorting activity.

Flannel-Board Patterns

RAIN ON MARS: Flannel-Board Patterns

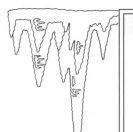

THE ICE STORM
(A Choral Chant)

The storm last night was made of ice,

Was made of ice, was made of ice.

It's clear as glass,

It looks so nice!

It looks so nice today.

It turned the roads to giant slides,

To giant slides, to giant slides.

Instead of walking,

We must glide!

We must glide today.

Choral Chant Directions

First, teach the words of "The Ice Storm" to the students and then have everyone sing the song to the tune of "Oh, Do You Know the Muffin Man?"

Follow-up Activities

"Break the ice" with ice cube treasures! Freeze trays of ice cubes with tiny plastic toys or charms, one in each cube. Students can observe how ice melts while they wait for their treasures to emerge.

Complete the reproducible activity, "The Ice Storm: Drawing Fun Page" on page 55.

THE ICE STORM: Drawing Fun Page

Directions: This page shows that an ice storm has come. Have the students color the page and add their own details so they can "be" in the ice storm story.

THE CONTEST
(A Play/Skit)

First student: The sun said, "My weather is the best!
I make people smile as I set in the west."

Second student: The rain said, "Without me, nothing could grow.
That must mean that I am the best, you know!"

Third student: The wind said, "I blow away leaves and dust.
A fresh, clean world is really a must."

Fourth student: The frost said, "But I am the only one
Who paints the leaves when summer is done!"

Fifth student: The snow said, "I think that I win today.
I'm the favorite weather for fun and play!"

Play/Skit Directions

Divide the class into groups of five or six students and assign a weather part to each child. Have each group perform the play. If you like, one student can be the narrator and will recite all of the parts of the sentences that are not within quotation marks, such as: the sun said, the rain said, etc.

Follow-up Activities

Have the class vote on their favorite kind of weather. Then post the results of the contest! Reduce the size of the paper bag puppet faces on page 57. Paste the faces onto a bar graph to represent each vote.

Complete the reproducible activity, "The Contest: Paper-Bag Puppets" found on page 57. The students can use the paper bag puppets to perform the play, "The Contest."

THE CONTEST: Paper-Bag Puppets

Directions: Make paper-bag puppets for the students, one for each part in the play. Students can perform a puppet show as an alternative to acting in the play. Color and cut out the faces from the pattern page and glue them to paper lunch bags. Add other details with craft supplies.

THE LOST BALL

(A Minibook Poem)

A big wind today
Blew my ball away.

It bounced on a train.
Then it started to rain.

My ball floated away,
In a puddle it stayed.

When the puddle dried up,
Along came a pup.

He ran to a log
With my ball in the fog!

He lost my red ball
And it rolled, in a fall,

Past the big town,
All the way down

The hill to my street
And right up to my feet!

Directions: Read this poem to the students before they begin work on their minibooks. Copy pages 58, 59, and 60 for each student. Have the students color, cut out, and staple the pages together in numerical order.

The Lost Ball

This minibook belongs to:

_____

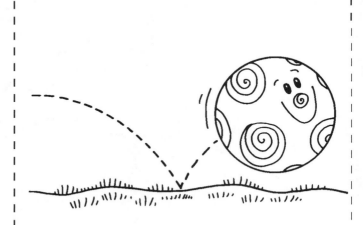

A big wind today
Blew my ball away.

-1-

It bounced on a train.
Then it started to rain.

-2-

My ball floated away,
In a puddle it stayed.

-3-

When the puddle dried up,
Along came a pup.

-4-

He ran to a log
With my ball in the fog!

-5-

He lost my red ball
And it rolled, in a fall,

-6-

Past the big town,
All the way down

-7-

The hill to my street
And right up to my feet!

-8-

Follow-up Activities

1. Make collages. Have each student look through magazines to find pictures of people playing sports, pets with toy balls, children with beach balls, etc. Then cut out circles from construction paper. Have the students glue their pictures onto the paper "balls."

2. Have a "lost ball" buffet. Make a list of foods that are circles and spheres—oranges, cookies, radishes, English muffins, pancakes, etc. Gather some of these foods and have the students enjoy this shape-oriented snack.

3. Talk about the weather in the story: wind, rain, fog, and then sunshine. Look for clues in the words of the poem and in the minibook pictures.

4. Brainstorm rhyming words! Start with the pairs of rhyming words in the poem: town/down; today/away; train/rain; up/pup; log/fog; ball/fall; street/feet. Choose one rime and see if students can come up with other words. For example, ball/fall: all, call, hall, mall, stall, wall. Write each word so the students can see it. Make a "Lost Ball" bulletin board with your brainstormed word lists.

PURPLE MONSTERS
(An Act-It-Out Poem)

Three purple monsters
Students hold up three fingers.

Bounced down the road.
Students bounce up and down in place.

They ate their purple lunches,
Students pretend to eat.

They talked in purple code.
*Students talk in a nonsense
language and wave hands.*

They laughed their purple laughs
Students laugh uproariously!

And nodded purple heads.
Students nod heads vigorously.

**And then they
Bounced back up the road**
Students bounce in place again.

To sleep in purple beds.
Students pretend to sleep.

Act-It-Out Poem Directions

Read the poem aloud while the students perform the suggested actions. This is also a fun stick-puppet rhyme. Copy the monster pattern found on page 62 and make three copies for each student. Students can color, cut out, and attach each monster to a craft stick using glue or double-sided tape. The monster patterns can also be glued to the front of lunch-size paper bags and used as hand puppets.

Follow-up Activities

Invite students to vote for their favorite purple things! Have students draw pictures of the objects they picked and then display the drawings on a bulletin board celebrating the color purple.

On page 63, you will find the reproducible activity, "Purple Monsters: Maze Fun Page." The children will delight in helping the monsters find their beds.

PURPLE MONSTERS:
Stick- or Paper-Bag Pattern

PURPLE MONSTERS: Maze Fun Page

Directions: Help the monsters get home to their beds! Say each picture word out loud. Pick the path that has rhyming words.

THE PINK PIG

(A Stick-Puppet Rhyme)

The pig danced with the roses,
As they swayed like pretty maids.
He touched three kittens' noses,
And drank pink lemonade.
He ate some cherry ice cream
Under a cherry tree,
And said, "The best things in the world—
They are all pink, like me!"

Stick-Puppet Directions

Use the stick puppet patterns on pages 64 and 65 to help tell the story of this poem. Copy, color, and cut out each pattern. Attach each figure to a craft stick using glue or double-sided tape.

Follow-up Activity

Make picture-word cards for words that rhyme with pink: sink, blink, ink, mink, rink, drink, think, etc. Help students create a "pink" song or poem that uses all "-ink" rime words.

Stick-Puppet Patterns

THE PINK PIG: Stick-Puppet Patterns

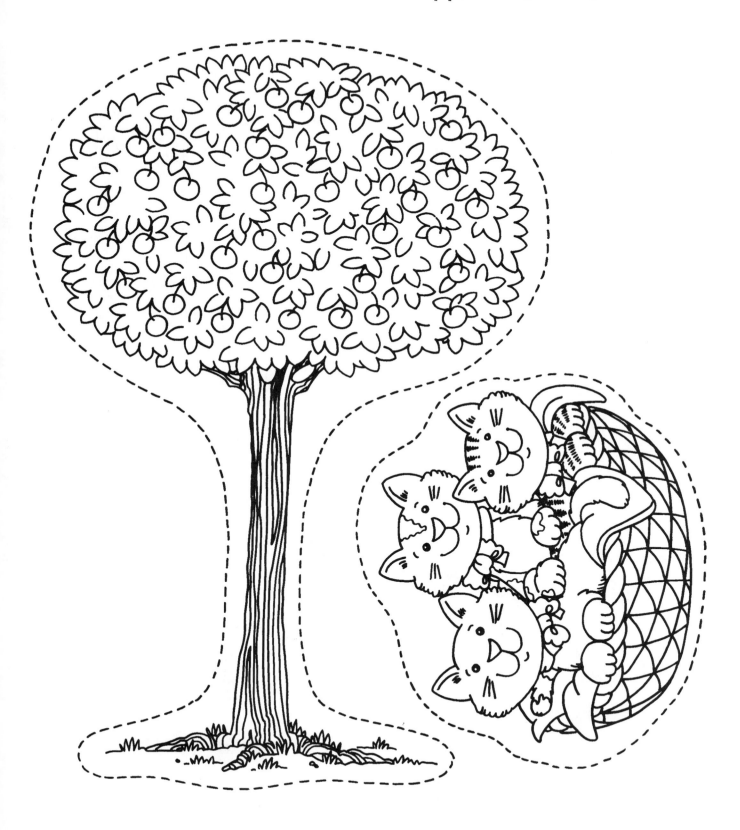

MYSTERY MEAL
(A Choral Chant)

For my birthday, as a treat,
My mom made me things to eat:
Crisp fish sticks and french fries,
Corn with butter, lemon pies,
Apple juice! Apple juice!

My favorite color—can you guess?
If you can, then yell out "Yes!"
Say the color loudly,
Say the color proudly,
Say it now! Say it now!

Choral Chant Directions

Teach the words of "Mystery Meal" to the students and then have everyone sing the song to the tune of "Frére Jacques."

Follow-up Activities

Make a lemon pie chart! Talk about your students' favorite yellow foods. Take a vote on the students' favorite foods, using either the food from the poem or other foods suggested by your students. Then show the results on the chart.

On page 67 you will find the reproducible activity, "Mystery Meal: Drawing Fun Page." Students will enjoy adding extra touches to the special birthday meal.

MYSTERY MEAL: Drawing Fun Page

Directions: This page shows the birthday meal from the poem. Ask the students to color the page and add their own birthday treats—as long as they are yellow!

THE BEAUTY OF BLUE
(A Flannel-Board Rhyme)

The deep, blue sea,
The bright, blue sky,
My blue beach ball,
This berry pie.
Some people say
"I'm blue" when sad.
But blue things always
Make ME glad!

Flannel-Board Rhyme Directions

This poem can be read aloud as you use the pattern pieces on the flannel board to reinforce different vocabulary words. The flannel-board patterns can be found on pages 68 and 69. Copy the patterns onto card stock, color, cut out, and laminate for durability. Then glue sandpaper or place self-stick Velcro™ on the back of each pattern.

Follow-up Activity

Play a rhyming trip game. Start with "I'm going to the beach and I'm going to take…" Encourage the students to think of objects that rhyme with the word "beach," such as peach, bleach, speech, etc. Then continue the game by saying, for example, "I'm going to take my beach ball and . . ." as students think up words that rhyme with "ball."

Flannel-Board Patterns

THE BEAUTY OF BLUE: Flannel-Board Patterns

LITTLE BROWN SPARROWS
(A Finger Play)

One little sparrow said to his wife,
"I'm sick and tired of our dark brown life!"
Students hold up one finger.

Two little sparrows said, "Let's find some paint!"
Students hold up two fingers.

Three little sparrows said, "Paint me and I'll faint!"
Students hold up three fingers.

Four little sparrows said, "Please stop and think!
Students hold up four fingers.

Cats could catch us if we all were pink!"
Students make whiskers with fingers.

Five little sparrows said, "Our color brown
Keeps us safe here and when we're in town."
Students hold up five fingers.

Then all the little sparrows cheered, "Hooray for brown!"
Students wave hands in the air and cheer.

Finger Play Directions

Read the poem aloud as the students perform the actions.

Follow-up Activities

Watch sparrows on your playground or at a nearby park. Can students count the sparrows? What else do they notice about them?

On page 71 you will find the reproducible activity, "Little Brown Sparrows: Sorting Activity." Students will love this "math" activity that will reinforce the rhyme.

LITTLE BROWN SPARROWS: Sorting Activity

Directions: Here are the little sparrows from the poem! See how many different ways the students can sort the sparrows. Copy and cut them out. Make two sorting circles with long pieces of yarn. Have the students talk about the sparrow pictures and sort and re-sort according to attributes (wearing a hat or not; wearing a scarf or not; singing or not; or going left or right). After the students sort for each attribute, ask them to count the number of sparrows in each set.

THE LOST BLACK CAT
(A Choral Chant)

High voices:	The coal-black cat With eyes so bright	Medium voices:	And found it had Its door ajar.
Medium voices:	Padded through The ink-black night.	High voices:	He leaped inside And fell asleep,
Low voices:	He saw a black, Abandoned car	Low voices:	Curled up on Its jet black seat.

Stick-Puppet Pattern

Choral Chant Directions

This choral chant uses different types of voices to make "music." Sort your students by the range of their voices. Assign appropriate lines for each group to learn. You can direct the poem like a piece of music.

Use the black cat pattern on this page to help tell the story of this poem. Copy, color, and cut out the pattern. Attach the cat onto a craft stick using glue or double-sided tape.

Follow-up Activity

Talk about lost pets. Animal shelters are places where lost pets can live until their owners find them again. Sometimes these pets are adopted by new families. Contact or visit an animal shelter to learn of other ways to help.

FIVE GREEN FROGS
(A Finger Play)

Five green frogs
Students hold up five fingers.

On three lily pads,
Students hold up three fingers.

Looking for their moms, looking for their dads.
Students shade their eyes with one hand and look around.

One said, "Look! A big, green blob.
Students point in same direction.

I think that's my mom
Or maybe Cousin Bob."
Students nod, then shake heads to show indecision.

All the frogs said,
"Let's swim over there!"
Students make swimming motions with hands.

They splashed in green water
From the fresh, green air.
Students make "splash" gestures
as if splashing water with hands.

Hear them splash as they dive:
One green, two green, three, four, five!
Students hold up one, two, three,
four, and then five fingers in turn.

Finger Play Directions
Read the poem aloud as the students perform the actions. The students will also enjoy making a frog mask to wear as they say the rhyme. The frog mask pattern is found on page 74.

Follow-up Activity
Show the students pictures of all kinds of frogs and talk about the variety of sizes, shapes, and colors. Then ask students to draw pictures of their favorite frogs. Combine the drawings in a classroom book called "Our Favorite Frogs."

FIVE GREEN FROGS: Frog Mask

Directions: Students can wear this mask for the finger play, "Five Green Frogs." Reproduce the mask on card stock for each student. Have the students color and cut out their masks. Then carefully cut out the eyeholes and the holes on each edge of the mask. Thread yarn or shoelaces through the holes so that the mask can be gently tied around the back.

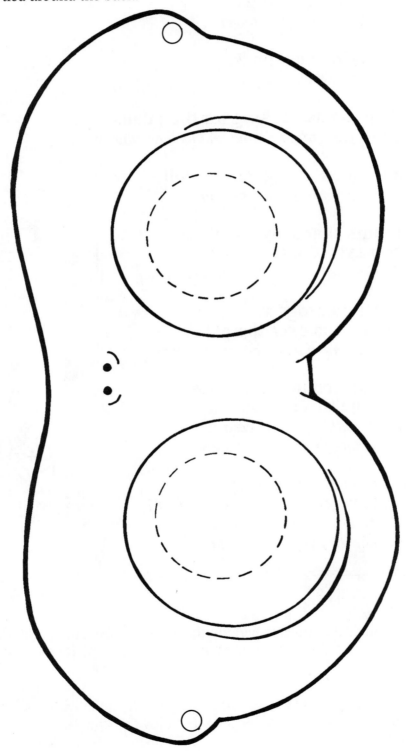

I LOVE RED
(An Act-It-Out Poem)

I dyed my hair red,
Students fluff up hair with fingers.

Put red sheets on the bed,
Students pretend to make a bed.

Put red paint on the door,
The walls, and the floor.
Students vigorously paint pretend doors, walls, floors!

Then I got new red chairs,
Students pretend to sit down.

And bright new red stairs,
Students pretend to climb stairs.

Red toys and red books—
Students pretend to play with toys or read books.

I got lots of looks!
Students look as if they are surprised.

But when you come to
My red house to view,
Students shade eyes as if viewing something in distance.

Can you see me,
As red as can be?
Students point to themselves.

Act-it-Out Poem Directions: Read the poem aloud while the students perform the suggested actions.

Follow-Up Activity
   On page 76 you will find the reproducible activity, "I Love Red: Coloring Sheet." Students will identify the color red in everyday objects.

I LOVE RED: Coloring Sheet

Directions: Some things don't have to be painted red—they already are red! Hand out this sheet and first have the students color only the red items. Then ask the students to use a variety of colors for the remaining items in each picture.

Which one is red?

Which one is red?

Which one is red?

Which one is red?

A FEAST IN SPACE
(A Play/Skit)

First student:	On Mercury, milk is bright, bright blue.
Second student:	On Venus, we love our purple stew!
Third student:	Here on the moon, we eat green cheese.
Fourth student:	On Mars, we grow red peas with ease.
Fifth student:	On Jupiter, we love gray fish sticks!
Sixth student:	On Saturn, we make green trail mix.
All students:	Our lovely dishes are a treat,
	And colors make them fun to eat!

Play/Skit Directions

Divide the class into groups of six and assign a part to each student. Have each group perform the play for the rest of the class.

Follow-up Activities

Look at a chart of the solar system. Have the students find the planets named in this play. Make a mobile of the planets. Cut out planet shapes from construction paper, punch a hole in each planet and tie the planets with yarn to straws or sticks.

Follow-up Activity

Invite the students to bake "Our New Planet Cookies." Purchase pre-made sugar cookie dough and bake following the directions on the package. Have the children add raisins, nuts, and chocolate chips as well as pressing small craters into the dough. The finished cookies will look like a new planet. Discuss the exciting discovery of the newest planet found in the summer of 2005.

A MESS AT THE ZOO
(A Minibook Poem)

The blue kangaroo
And the brown and gold parrot
Brought the orange rabbit
A bright purple carrot.
The tall, red giraffe
Told the green and tan lion,
"I watched those pink monkeys—
Yes, I have been spying!
They climbed and they climbed
And laughed all day, too,
Spilling buckets of paint
All over the zoo!"

Minibook Poem Directions:

Read this poem to the students before they begin work on their minibooks. Copy pages 78, 79, and 80 for each student. Have the students color, cut out, and staple the pages together in numerical order.

A Mess at the Zoo

This minibook belongs to:

_____

The blue kangaroo

-1-

And the brown
and gold parrot

-2-

Brought the orange rabbit
A bright purple carrot.

-3-

The tall, red giraffe

-4-

Told the green and tan lion,

-5-

"I watched those
pink monkeys —
Yes, I have been spying!

-6-

They climbed and they climbed
And laughed all day, too,

-7-

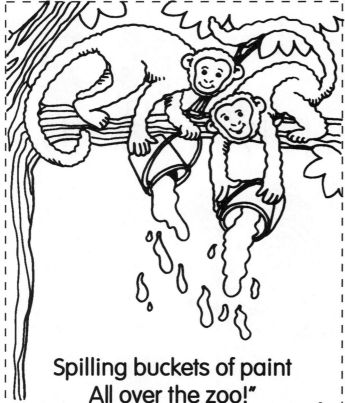

Spilling buckets of paint
All over the zoo!"

-8-

Follow-up Activities

1. Make a zoo color wheel. Look at pictures of real zoo animals. What colors do the students see? From the golden-brown of a lion to the red and blue feathers of a parrot, there are plenty of colors at the zoo! You can create a pie-chart "color wheel" with the students. Write the names of the animals that share each color in the wedges of your pie chart.

2. Take a break with a zoo-appropriate snack. Have milk and animal crackers. Ask the students to identify their crackers as they snack!

3. If you can, take a field-trip to the zoo. Or, "visit" a zoo with a virtual tour. Many zoos in the United States have web sites with fun features such as live cameras that show the animals.

4. Play a zoo rhyming game! Make up funny names for the animals in the zoo. The "first" name of the animal has to rhyme with its "last name," which identifies what type of animal it is. Here are some ideas to get you started: Brian Lion, Neil Seal, Pauline Wolverine, Bunky Monkey, etc. Or use attributes for the first name: Chunky Monkey, Sighin' Lion, etc.

VALENTINE SWIMMING PARTY
(A Choral Chant)

I made some lacey little hearts,
Little hearts, little hearts,
I took my lacey little hearts
To give away at school.

Then I dropped my little hearts,
Little hearts, little hearts,
As I walked to class that day
I dropped them in the pool!

When I got to class that day,
Class that day, class that day,
All my friends laughed and played
To see hearts in the pool!

We got our swimsuits and we dove,
And we dove, and we dove,
Into that heart-filled treasure trove
In the pool at school!

Choral Chant Directions

First teach the words of "Valentine Swimming Party" to the students and then have everyone sing the song to the tune of "Mary Had a Little Lamb."

Follow-up Activities

Take a few minutes on Valentine's Day to talk about the human heart. What keeps our hearts healthy? Do Valentine's jumping jacks and running in place to show our hearts that we love them!

On page 82 you will find the reproducible activity, "Valentine Swimming Party: Valentines for Everybody!" Students can make Valentines to share with their friends.

VALENTINE SWIMMING PARTY:
Valentines for Everybody!

You will need: Sheets of red, pink, and white paper; red and pink crayons or markers; glitter, lace edging, and stickers (optional).

Directions: Reproduce the pattern below on sheets of colored paper for the students. Have the students color and decorate their Valentines and write their friends' names on them. Then they may add stickers, glitter, or lace edging if desired. Students can make one or more Valentines to display or give away.

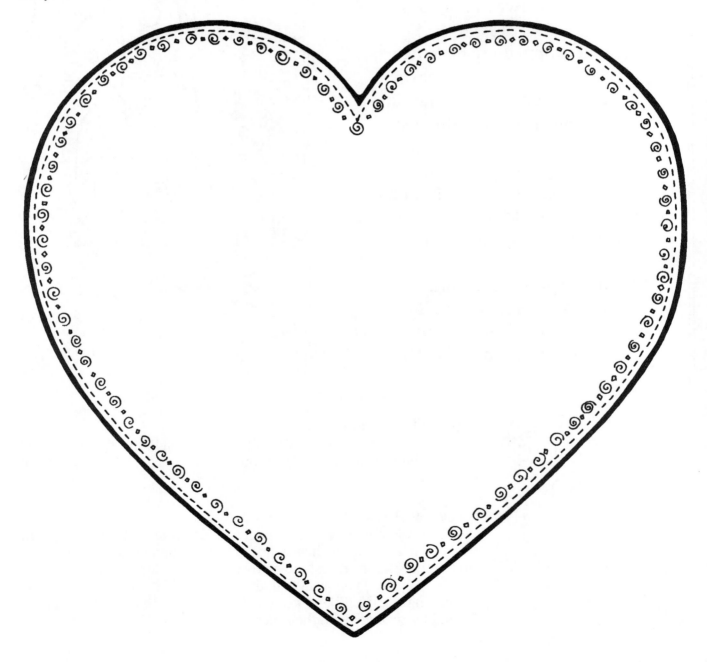

ARBOR DAY
(An Act-It-Out Poem)

All across the town,
People were planting trees,
Students should dig as if planting trees.

Evergreens and maples,
Oaks and Lombardies.
Students hold up arms for branches
and sway like trees in the wind.

All the birds were watching
As the people planted trees,
Students hop like birds.

Then they sang a sweet song
To show that they were pleased:
Students wave arms and pretend to sing.

"Thank you for these trees!
Students clasp hands in thanks.

Someday we'll build a nest here.
Students pretend to build nests.

Arbor Day is great,
Because trees are the best here!"
Students flap arms like wings and cheer.

Act-it-Out Poem Directions
Read the poem aloud while the students perform the suggested actions.

Follow-up Activities
Bring a seedling to class. Let the students take turns caring for it. Obtain permission to plant the seedling on school grounds and watch it start to grow! On page 84 you will find the reproducible activity, "Arbor Day: Learn about Trees."

ARBOR DAY: Learn about Trees.

Directions: Copy for each student. Talk about how trees grow and color the pictures.

Trees grow from seeds.

A seed is planted in the ground.

A tiny tree starts to grow.

The baby tree is called a seedling.

People can buy seedlings to plant.

People plant trees on Arbor Day.

MOTHER'S DAY IS EVERYWHERE!
(A Flannel-Board Rhyme)

Baby tigers all have moms,
So do baby bears.
Baby otters love their moms,
Baby birds love theirs!

Without mother ostriches,
Baby chicks can't grow.
Baby ducks stay close to Mom,
Because they love her so!

All the whole world over,
Baby lions, fish, and boars,
Love their loving mothers
Just like you love yours!

Flannel-Board Directions

Read this poem aloud as you use the pieces on the flannel board to reinforce different vocabulary words. Copy the patterns found on pages 85 and 86. Color, cut out, and laminate for durability. Glue sandpaper or place self-stick Velcro™ on the back of each pattern.

Follow-up Activity

Make Mother's Day cards from folded construction paper. If you like, you can reproduce the poem or the last stanza of the poem to glue inside each card. Have the students draw pictures of themselves with their mothers for the fronts of the cards.

Flannel-Board Patterns

MOTHER'S DAY IS EVERYWHERE!
Flannel-Board Patterns

PIE PICNIC
(A Stick-Puppet Poem)

For our picnic, Mom baked a pie.
So did Aunt Sara and Uncle Ty.
Aunt Min said, "I'll make pies with cherries!"
Uncle Fred baked a pie full of berries.
Cousin Sue said, "I'll bake lemon ones,
Pies as bright as the summer sun!"
Cousin Dan said, "I'll bring hot dogs and buns."
It's a good thing he thought that hot dogs were fun!
At our family picnic that warm July,
We each got one hot dog and pie, pie, pie!

Stick-Puppet Directions
Use the stick puppets to help tell the story of this poem. Patterns can be found on pages 87 and 88. Copy, color, and cut out each pattern. Attach each figure to a craft stick using glue or double-sided tape.

Follow-up Activity
Make picture-word cards for words that rhyme with pie: sky, eye, tie, fly, dry, etc. Try to make up a "pie" song or poem that uses all long-i rime words.

PIE PICNIC: Stick-Puppet Patterns

PARADE DAY
(An Act-It-Out Poem)

Oom-pah-pah, oom-pah-pah,
Students pretend to play trombones.

Here comes the band!
Students point in the distance.

Next, the red fire truck—

Isn't it grand?
Students make a fire-engine siren sound.

Look! There are funny clowns

Dancing around,
Students dance like silly clowns.

Followed by drummers—

Here that sharp sound?
Students march and pretend to play drums.

Rat-a-tat! Rat-a-tat!

Now clap your hands!
Students clap hands.

March to the sound of

The drums and the band.
Students march around the room,
pretending to play instruments.

Act-It-Out Poem Directions
Read the poem aloud while the students perform the suggested actions.

Follow-up Activities
Plan a parade! Make up a special occasion for a parade. Make badges or hats to wear. Hand out noisemakers for "instruments." Invite a crowd!

On page 90 you will find the reproducible activity, "Parade Day: Maze Fun." Students will delight in helping the parade find its way to the fire station.

PARADE DAY: Maze Fun

Directions: Help the parade march all the way to the fire station! Draw a line to show the way.

FIRST DAY OF SCHOOL

(A Play/Skit)

First student: Carla said, "See my new dress?"

Second student: Stanley said, "My desk is a mess!"

Third student: Rachel said, "I have vacation blues."

Fourth student: Tyler said, "I have brand-new shoes!"

Fifth student: Pip said, "Summer went way too fast."

Sixth student: Jamal said, "YAY! We're in class at last!"

Seventh student: Ms. Thompson said, "The time is here
To start our brand-new learning year."

Play/Skit Directions

Divide the class into groups of seven or eight and assign a part to each student. If you wish, you can also assign a narrator who speaks the part of each line that is outside of quotation marks: Carla said, Stanley said, etc. Have each group perform the skit for the rest of the class.

Follow-up Activities

Talk about the first day of school. What is fun about going back to school? What is difficult? Talk about how different people have different feelings, just like the students in the play.

On page 92 you will find the reproducible activity, "First Day of School: Count the Good Things!" This page can be used as a discussion starter as well as a fun coloring activity.

FIRST DAY OF SCHOOL: Count the Good Things!

Directions: Discuss each good thing about starting a new year at school. Have the students circle what they like best. Then ask them to color the page.

new books

new friends

new teacher

new classroom

new school supplies

new things to learn

HALLOWEEN
(An Act-It-Out Poem)

The moon is out; it's full and bright.
Students hold up arms to make a round moon.

Tonight is an exciting night!
Students wave hands excitedly.

The moon shines down on the spooky town.
Students make fluttering gestures with fingers to show "shining down."

We creep to doors and jump up and down.
Students jump up and down.

We get to yell out "TRICK OR TREAT!"
Students yell.

Then people give us things to eat—
Students rub stomachs.

Bright red apples, sweet and crunchy,
Students pretend to eat apples.

Chocolate bars, nice and munchy!
Students peel open pretend candy bars.

Kids dressed as bats and scary bears,
Students look scary and yell "Boo!"

Cats, robots, and pumpkins are everywhere!
Students point all around room to show "everywhere."

Act-It-Out Poem Directions
Read the poem aloud while the students perform the suggested actions.

Follow-up Activities
Make a list of everybody's favorite Halloween treats. Look for pictures of the treats in magazines. Make a class collage to display on a bulletin board. On page 94 you will find the reproducible activity, "Halloween: Trick-or-Treat Mask."

HALLOWEEN: Trick-or-Treat Mask

Directions: Students can wear this mask for the Act-it-Out poem, "Halloween." Reproduce the mask on card stock for each child. Have the students color and cut out their masks. Then carefully cut out the eyeholes and the holes on each edge of the mask. Thread yarn or shoelaces through the holes so that the mask can be gently tied around the back of the head.

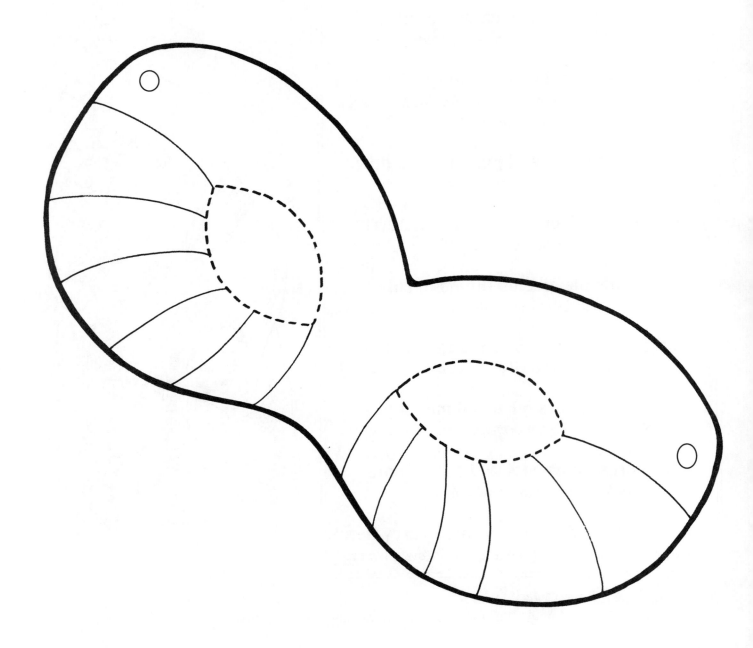

TURKEY CAROL
(A Choral Chant)

O great big turkey on the stove,
How golden-brown you are!
O pies so sweet, you are a treat,
And gravy, you're the star!
I love Thanksgiving dinner,
From yams to ham to corn,
After we eat, put up your feet,
And snooze until the morn!

Choral Chant Directions
First teach the words of "Turkey Carol" to the students and then have everyone sing the song to the tune of "O Little Town of Bethlehem."

Follow-up Activity
Brainstorm pairs of rhyming words that relate to Thanksgiving and cooking Thanksgiving dinner. Some examples include: peas, teas; pie, fry; ham, jam; dressing, blessing; potatoes, tomatoes; dish, fish, etc.

Turkey Pattern Below
Copy the turkey pattern below for each student. Color, cut out, and attach to a craft stick using glue or double-sided tape. Encourage the students to make up their own "turkey rhymes."

SANTA'S ELVES
(A Finger Play)

The elves are busy every day
Making toys for Santa's sleigh.
Students make hammering motions.

Do you wonder what they do?
I will make a list for you!
Students pretend to write out a list.

They put wheels on cars
Students pretend to roll a toy car.

Paint toy drums with stars
Students pretend to paint.

Draw doll faces
Students pretend to draw a smiling face.

Build tracks for races
Students pretend to put together pieces of track.

Put letters on blocks
Students draw letters in the air with finger.

Knit mittens and socks
Students pretend to knit.

Sew cuddly cats
Students pretend to sew.

Carve baseball bats
Students pretend to carve wood.

Make peppermint candy—
Students pretend to pop candy into mouths.

Now, aren't those elves handy?

Finger Play Directions
Read the poem aloud as students perform the finger play actions.

SANTA'S ELVES: Rhyming Riddles

Directions: To reinforce the learning of rhyming words, tell these fun riddles from Santa's workshop. Explain to your students that the answers have to rhyme. To reinforce visual learning of the words make picture word cards of the following answers: *shelves, day, eve, and seat.*

1. Where do Santa's elves put their hats?
   on elves' _____

2. What is the special date when the elves paint Santa's sleigh?
   sleigh _____

3. What do the elves call the night when Santa leaves with the toys?
   leave _____

4. What would you call a carefully made chair by an elf?
   a neat _____